ENGLISH

VISUAL DICTIONARY

T0313589

Published by Collins
An imprint of HarperCollins Publishers
Westerhill Road
Bishopbriggs
Glasgow G64 2QT

HarperCollins Publishers, Macken House,
39/40 Mayor Street Upper, Dublin 1,
D01 C9W8, Ireland

First Edition 2020

10 9 8 7

© HarperCollins Publishers 2020

ISBN 978-0-00-837227-9

Collins® is a registered trademark of
HarperCollins Publishers Limited

Typeset by Jouve, India

Printed in India

Acknowledgements
We would like to thank those authors and
publishers who kindly gave permission for
copyright material to be used in the Collins
Corpus. We would also like to thank Times
Newspapers Ltd for providing valuable data.

A catalogue record for this book is available
from the British Library

If you would like to comment on any aspect
of this book, please contact us at the given
address or online.
E-mail dictionaries@harpercollins.co.uk
 www.facebook.com/collinsdictionary
 @collinsdict

MANAGING EDITOR
Maree Airlie

FOR THE PUBLISHER
Gerry Breslin
Robin Scrimgeour

CONTRIBUTORS
Rebecca Adlard

MIX
Paper | Supporting
responsible forestry
FSC™ C007454

This book is produced from independently certified FSC™ paper
to ensure responsible forest management.

For more information visit: www.harpercollins.co.uk/green

CONTENTS

INTRODUCTION

Whether you're on holiday or staying in the UK for a longer time, your **Collins Visual Dictionary** will help you with the words you need, when you need them. With over a thousand clear and helpful images, you can quickly find the vocabulary you are looking for.

The Collins Visual Dictionary includes:

- 10 **chapters** arranged by theme, so that you can easily find what you need for each situation
- **images** – illustrating the essential items you might need
- **YOU MIGHT SAY...** – common phrases that you might want to use
- **YOU MIGHT HEAR...** – common phrases that you might come across
- **VOCABULARY** – common words that you might need to know
- **YOU SHOULD KNOW...** – tips about local customs
- an **index** to find all images quickly and easily
- essential **phrases** and **numbers** listed on the flaps for quick reference

USING YOUR COLLINS VISUAL DICTIONARY

In order to make sure that the phrases and vocabulary in the **Collins Visual Dictionary** are given in a way that's clear and easy to understand, we have followed certain policies:

1) All plural words have been marked with the plural marker, for example, **herbs** *pl*.

2) Where they are different, feminine forms of nouns have been shown after the masculine form, for example, **waiter/waitress**. Where only one form has been shown, that form is used for both men and women, for example, **firefighter**.

3) Verbs are shown in the "to" infinitive form, for example, **to change trains**.

FREE AUDIO

We have created a free audio resource to help you learn and practise the words for all of the images shown in this dictionary. The words in each chapter are spoken by native speakers, giving you the opportunity to listen to each word twice and repeat it yourself. Download the audio from:
www.collinsdictionary.com/resources

THE ESSENTIALS

If you visit the UK, or perhaps live there, you will want to chat with people, and get to know them better. The more language you have, the more confident in English you will become.

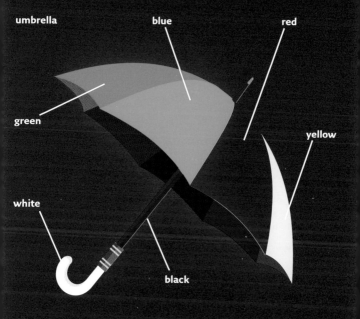

umbrella

blue

red

green

yellow

white

black

It is polite to use "Mr/Mrs/Ms" when you are talking to people you don't know very well. "Mr" is used for all men; "Mrs" is used for a married woman; and "Ms" can be used for any woman, married or not. "Miss" is mainly used for girls.

Hello.	Good night.	See you soon.
Hi!	How do you do?	See you tomorrow.
Good morning.	Pleased to meet you.	See you on Saturday.
Good afternoon.	Goodbye.	Have a good day!
Good evening.	Bye!	Have a good evening!

YOU SHOULD KNOW...

British people often shake hands when they first meet. Friends and relatives usually give each other a hug, or perhaps a kiss on the cheek.

Yes.	Thank you.	I'm sorry.
No.	No, thanks.	OK!
I don't know.	Excuse me.	You're welcome.
please	Sorry?	I don't understand.

YOU SHOULD KNOW...

When someone says "Sorry?" as a question, it means they would like you to repeat what you've said.

What's your name?	I'm ... (years old).	I live in...
My name is...	Where are you from?	I'm from Russia/Turkey.
How old are you?	Where do you live?	I'm Russian/Turkish.

YOU SHOULD KNOW...

It is not polite in the UK to ask an adult how old they are.

FRIENDS AND FAMILY

This is my...

These are my...

husband

wife

son

daughter

parents *pl*

partner

boyfriend

girlfriend

fiancé/fiancée

father

mother

brother

sister

grandparents *pl*

grandfather

grandmother

grandson

granddaughter

father-in-law

mother-in-law

daughter-in-law

son-in-law

brother-in-law

sister-in-law

stepfather

stepmother

stepbrother

stepsister

stepson

stepdaughter

uncle

aunt

nephew

niece

cousin

friend

baby

child

teenager

Are you married/single?

I'm married/single.

I'm divorced.

I have a partner.

I'm widowed.

Do you have any children?

I have ... children.

I don't have any children.

How are you?

How's it going?

How is he/she?

How are they?

Very well, thanks, and you?

Fine, thanks.

Great!

I'm OK.

Not bad, thanks.

I'm tired.

I'm thirsty.

I'm hungry.

I'm full.

I'm cold.

I'm warm.

I am...

You are...

He/She is

They/We are...

happy

excited

surprised

angry

sad

worried

afraid

bored

I feel...

You feel...

He/She feels...

They/We feel...

well

better

worse

Where do you work?

What do you do?

What's your occupation?

Do you work/study?

I'm self-employed.

I'm unemployed.

I'm still at school.

I'm at university.

I'm retired.

I'm travelling.

I have my own business.

I work part-/full-time.

I work as a/an...

I'm a/an...

architect

builder

chef

cleaner

dentist

doctor

driver

electrician

engineer

farmer

firefighter

fisherman

IT worker

joiner

journalist

lawyer

mechanic

nurse

office worker

plumber

police officer

postal worker

sailor

salesperson

scientist

soldier

teacher

vet

waiter/waitress

I work at/for/in...

business

company

construction site

factory

government

hospital

hotel

office

restaurant

school

shop

morning	a.m.	When...?
afternoon	p.m.	... in 60 seconds/two minutes.
evening	What time is it?	... in quarter of an hour/half an hour.
night	It's nine o'clock.	
midday	It's ten past nine.	... in an hour.
midnight	It's quarter past nine.	early
today	It's 25 past nine.	late
tonight	It's half past nine.	soon
tomorrow	It's 20 to ten.	later
yesterday	It's quarter to ten.	now
the day after tomorrow	It's five to ten.	before
the day before yesterday	It's 17:30.	after

YOU SHOULD KNOW...

In the UK, people don't usually use the 24-hour clock to talk about the time.

Monday	Wednesday	Friday	Sunday
Tuesday	Thursday	Saturday	

January	April	July	October
February	May	August	November
March	June	September	December

spring	summer	autumn	winter

day	weekly	the week before
weekend	monthly	the week after
week	yearly	in February
fortnight	on Mondays	in 2019
month	every Sunday	in the '80s
year	last Thursday	in spring
daily	next Friday	in winter

What's the weather like?	It's snowing.	sunny
	It's windy.	sun
What's the temperature?	It is...	rain
How warm/cold is it?	nice	snow
Is it going to rain?	horrible	wind
What a lovely day!	hot	fog
It's cloudy.	warm	thunderstorm
It's raining.	wet	cloud

TRANSPORT

There are lots of ways to get to the UK and to travel around the country. There are many good roads and motorways, as well as railways that go up, down and across the country, and airports in many of the bigger towns and cities. Ferries also travel to a lot of European places, and take passengers to the many islands off the British coast.

black cab

light

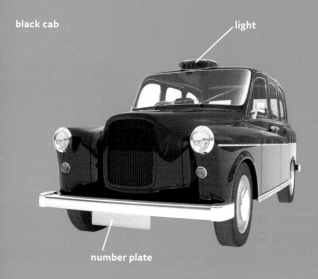

number plate

When you ask someone for directions, first say "Excuse me", then ask for the information you want. The person might say how far the place is in either yards and miles, or metres and kilometres.

YOU MIGHT SAY...

Excuse me...

Where is...?

Which way is...?

What's the quickest way to...?

How far away is it?

Is it far from here?

I'm lost.

I'm looking for...

I'm going to...

Can I walk there?

YOU MIGHT HEAR...

It's over there.

It's in the other direction.

It's ... miles/minutes away.

Go straight ahead.

Turn left/right.

It's next to...

It's opposite...

It's near to...

Follow the signs for...

That's ... pounds, please.

VOCABULARY

traffic	directions *pl*	to return
rush hour	to walk	to cross
public transport	to drive	to turn

YOU SHOULD KNOW...

At traffic lights, an amber light signals to traffic that a change is about to happen. Pedestrians should not cross the road while the amber light is on. Remember to look right before you cross.

driver

map

passenger

pedestrian

road sign

street

taxi

taxi meter

taxi rank

ticket

timetable

traffic lights *pl*

Traffic drives on the left-hand side in the UK. Remember to carry your driving licence and insurance documents while driving.

YOU MIGHT SAY...	YOU MIGHT HEAR...
Is this the road to...?	You can/can't park here.
Can I park here?	It's free to park here.
Do I have to pay to park?	It costs ... to park here.
I'd like to hire a car.	Car hire is ... per day/week.
How much is it per day/week?	May I see your documents, please?
When/Where must I return it?	Which pump are you at?
Where is the nearest petrol station?	How much fuel would you like?

YOU SHOULD KNOW...

If you are in the UK for more than 12 months and you want to drive, you must change your non-UK driving licence for a British one.

VOCABULARY

passenger seat	clutch	hybrid
driver's seat	air conditioning	to start the engine
back seat	cruise control	to brake
engine	manual	to slow down
brake	automatic	to speed
accelerator	electric	to stop

YOU SHOULD KNOW...

There are drink-driving laws in the UK; you should not drink and drive.

battery

Breathalyser®

caravan

child seat

motorhome

people carrier

roof rack

sunroof

SUV

to overtake

to park

to reverse

dashboard

fuel gauge

gear stick

glove compartment

handbrake

headrest

ignition

rearview mirror

sat nav

seatbelt

speedometer

steering wheel

boot   roof   window

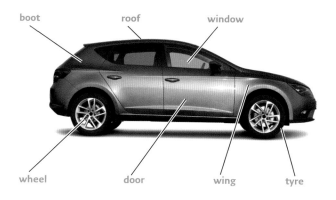

wheel   door   wing   tyre

windscreen wiper   wing mirror

windscreen

bonnet

bumper

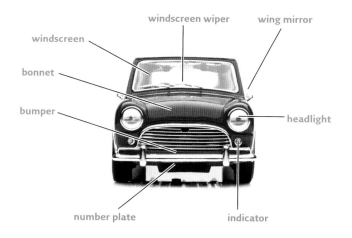

headlight

number plate   indicator

In the UK, the speed limit is usually 70 mph (112 kmph) on motorways, 60 mph (96 kmph) on main roads, and 30 mph (48 kmph) in towns and cities. You have to pay for some roads and bridges, and in London you have to pay to drive into the city centre.

VOCABULARY

dual carriageway	hard shoulder	car hire/rental
corner	services *pl*	rental car
exit	driving licence	unleaded petrol
slip road	car insurance	diesel

YOU SHOULD KNOW...

Double yellow lines on the road means no parking at any time.

accessible parking space

bridge

car park

car wash

diversion

double yellow lines *pl*

fuel pump

junction

kerb

lane

layby

level crossing

motorway

parking meter

parking space

pavement

pedestrian crossing

petrol station

pothole

road

roadworks *pl*

roundabout

single-track road

speed camera

speed limit

toll

traffic cone

traffic jam

traffic warden

tunnel

CAR TROUBLE

If you break down and your car stops working on the motorway, you can call the police or a breakdown service using one of the orange emergency telephones at the side of the road. Get out of your car and stand a little way away from it while you wait for help.

YOU MIGHT SAY...

Can you help me?

I've broken down.

I've had an accident.

I've run out of petrol.

I've got a flat tyre.

I've lost my car keys.

The car won't start.

There's a problem with...

Call an ambulance/the police.

Is there a garage/petrol station near here?

Can you help me change this wheel?

When will the car be fixed?

May I take your details?

YOU MIGHT HEAR...

Do you need any help?

Are you hurt?

What's wrong with your car?

Where have you broken down?

It will cost...

The car will be ready by...

I need to take your details.

YOU SHOULD KNOW...

It is useful to keep items such as a warning triangle, hi-viz vest, and jump leads in your car.

accident	hazard lights *pl*	to have a flat tyre
breakdown	to have an accident	to run out of petrol

GENERAL

airbag

antifreeze

breakdown service

collision

de-icer

emergency phone

flat tyre

garage

hi-viz vest

(ice) scraper

jack

jump leads *pl*

mechanic

petrol can

snow shovel

spare wheel

tow truck

warning triangle

to break down

to change a tyre

to tow

BUS

Bus services in towns and cities are usually good; there are fewer buses in the country. Coaches take people on longer journeys from one city to another.

YOU MIGHT SAY...

Is there a bus to...?

When is the next bus to...?

Which bus goes to...?

Where is the bus stop?

Which stand does the coach leave from?

Where can I buy tickets?

How much is it to go to...?

A single/return, please.

Could you tell me when to get off?

How many stops is it?

I want to get off at the next stop, please.

YOU MIGHT HEAR...

The number 17 goes to...

The bus stop is...

It leaves from stand 21.

There's a bus every 10 minutes.

You can buy tickets at the office/on the bus.

This is your stop.

Have you got a bus pass?

VOCABULARY

bus route	concession	school bus
bus pass	day ticket	to catch the bus
fare	wheelchair access	to miss the bus

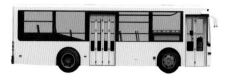

bus

bus lane

bus shelter

bus station

bus stop

coach

double-decker bus

minibus

shuttle bus

There are many cycling routes in the UK, both short- and long-distance. Some roads have cycle lanes, but otherwise cyclists must keep to the left-hand side of the road.

YOU MIGHT SAY...

Where can I hire a bicycle?

How much is it to hire a bike?

YOU MIGHT HEAR...

Bike hire is ... per day/week.

You must wear a helmet.

VOCABULARY

cyclist

cycle lane

cycle path

to cycle

to go for a bike ride

to get a puncture

GENERAL

bike rack

child seat

mountain bike

puncture

puncture repair kit

road bike

ACCESSORIES

bell

bike lock

helmet

lights *pl*

pump

reflective vest

BICYCLE

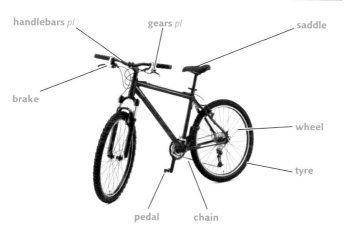

handlebars *pl*

gears *pl*

saddle

brake

wheel

tyre

pedal

chain

To ride a moped or motorcycle in the UK you must have a provisional licence and do a training course before you take your motorbike test. By law, motorcyclists must wear a helmet.

GENERAL

boots *pl*

helmet

helmet cam

leather gloves *pl*

leather jacket

moped

motorbike

motorcyclist

scooter

You can travel by rail across England, Scotland, Wales, and Northern Ireland. There are also rail connections to Europe via the Channel Tunnel. There are metro systems in London, Glasgow, and Newcastle, and trams operate in some cities, including Blackpool and Edinburgh.

YOU MIGHT SAY...

Is there a train to...?

When is the next train to...?

How many stops is it?

Which platform does it leave from?

Which line do I take for...?

A ticket to ..., please.

A single/return ticket to ..., please.

I'd like to reserve a seat, please.

Do I have to change?

Where do I change for...?

Where is platform 4?

Is this the right train/platform for...?

Is this seat free?

I've missed my train!

YOU MIGHT HEAR...

The next train leaves at...

Would you like a single or return ticket?

I'm sorry, this journey is fully booked.

You must change at...

Platform 4 is down there.

This is the right train/platform.

You have to go to platform 2.

This seat is free/taken.

Tickets, please.

The next stop is...

Change here for...

quiet coach	peak ticket	return ticket
aisle	off-peak ticket	e-ticket
railcard	single ticket	to change trains

YOU SHOULD KNOW...

You can buy your ticket before you travel, but you can also buy tickets on the train. Train tickets will cost more during busy morning and evening periods (peak times).

carriage

coach

departure board

first class

freight train

guard

left luggage locker

light railway

locomotive

luggage rack

metro

metro station

passenger train

platform

refreshments trolley

restaurant car

seat reservation

signal box

sleeper

sliding doors *pl*

ticket barrier

ticket machine

ticket office

toilets *pl*

track

train

train conductor

train station

tram

viaduct

The UK has many airports. Some airlines only fly at certain times of the year to and from the UK.

YOU MIGHT SAY...

I'm looking for check-in/my gate.

I'm checking in one bag.

Which gate does the plane leave from?

When does the gate open/close?

Is the flight on time?

I would like a window/an aisle seat, please.

I've lost my luggage.

My flight has been delayed.

I've missed my flight/connection.

Is there a shuttle bus service?

YOU MIGHT HEAR...

Check-in has opened for flight...

May I see your passport, please?

How many bags are you checking in?

Please go to gate number...

Your flight is on time/delayed.

Is this your bag?

Flight ... is now ready for boarding.

Last call for passenger...

VOCABULARY

airline	economy class	hold luggage
Arrivals/Departures	aisle	hold
Security	seatbelt	wing
Customs	hand luggage	jetlag
business class	oversize baggage	to check in (online)

aeroplane

airport

baggage reclaim

boarding card

cabin

cabin baggage

cabin crew

check-in desk

cockpit

departure board

duty-free shop

flight attendant

gate

lifejacket

luggage trolley

overhead locker

oxygen mask

passport

passport control

pilot

runway

suitcase

terminal

tray table

FERRY AND BOAT TRAVEL

A lot of ferries travel from the UK to Europe. Ferries also travel to the many islands around Britain.

YOU MIGHT SAY...

When is the next boat to...?

Where does the boat leave from?

What time is the last boat to...?

How long is the trip/crossing?

How many crossings a day are there?

How much for ... passengers?

How much is it for a vehicle?

YOU MIGHT HEAR...

The boat leaves from...

The trip/crossing lasts...

There are ... crossings a day.

The ferry is delayed/cancelled.

VOCABULARY

ferry crossing	coastguard	foot passenger
ferry terminal	lifeboat	to board
car deck	captain	to sail

YOU SHOULD KNOW...

The UK also has thousands of miles of canals and rivers. Many people enjoy travelling along the canals on canal boats, and some people even live on these boats.

anchor

buoy

canal

deck

harbour

lifebuoy

lifejacket

lock

marina

mooring

pier

port

canal boat

canoe

cruise ship

ferry

inflatable

kayak

rowing boat

sailing boat

yacht

IN THE HOME

Many people come to the UK for a holiday or for a longer stay if they are going to work or study. In the UK their home might be a city flat, a house in the country, or a family home in a town.

block of flats

roof

balcony

window

Many people in the UK live in the city. Often people go to the countryside at the weekend or for a holiday.

YOU MIGHT SAY...

I live in...

I'm staying at...

My address is...

I have a flat/house.

I'm moving to...

I'd like to buy/rent here.

YOU MIGHT HEAR...

Where do you live?

Where are you staying?

How long have you lived here?

What's your address, please?

Do you like this area?

Where are you moving to?

VOCABULARY

building	tenant	to rent
house	neighbour	to own
flat	deposit	to move house
address	mortgage	to buy
owner	rent	to sell

YOU SHOULD KNOW...

To rent a house or a flat in the UK go to an estate agent's office. They can help you.

block of flats

bungalow

cottage

detached house

farmhouse

high-rise block

semi-detached
house

studio flat

suburb

terraced house

townhouse

villa

YOU MIGHT SAY...

There's a problem with...

It's not working.

The drains are blocked.

The boiler has broken.

There's no hot water.

I need a plumber/
an electrician.

Can you recommend anyone?

Can you repair it?

I can smell gas/smoke.

YOU MIGHT HEAR...

What's the problem?

How long has it been broken/
blocked?

Where is the meter/fuse box?

Here's the number for a
plumber/an electrician.

VOCABULARY

room	floor	central heating
basement	balcony	to break
attic	electricity	to repair
ceiling	plumbing	to decorate
wall	air conditioning	to paint

YOU SHOULD KNOW...

The best way to find someone to repair something in your home in the UK is to ask a friend or neighbour if they know anybody who can help.

boiler

conservatory

extension cable

French windows

fuse box

heater

light bulb

meter

plug

radiator

satellite dish

security alarm

skylight

smoke alarm

socket

switch

thermostat

wood-burning stove

OUTSIDE

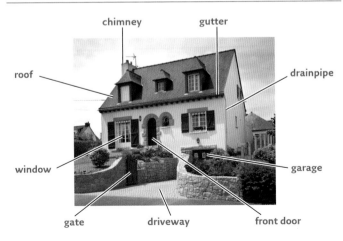

chimney

gutter

roof

drainpipe

window

garage

gate

driveway

front door

46

YOU MIGHT SAY/HEAR...

Would you like to come round?	Shall I take my shoes off?
Hi! Come in.	Can I use your bathroom?
Make yourself at home.	Thanks for inviting me.

VOCABULARY

stairs *pl*	lock	to wipe your feet
landing	to open/shut the door	to hang your jacket up
lift	to let somebody in	

YOU SHOULD KNOW...

If you are invited round to somebody's house, it is usually polite to take a small gift, such as flowers or a bottle of wine.

doorbell

doormat

intercom

key

letterbox

lift

VOCABULARY

carpet	cable TV	TV on demand
satellite TV	smart TV	to sit down

GENERAL

bookcase

curtains *pl*

display cabinet

DVD/Blu-ray® player

radio

remote control

sideboard

sofa bed

table lamp

TV stand

Venetian blind

voice assistant

to listen to music

to relax

to watch TV

LOUNGE

wall light   TV   fireplace   coffee table   sofa   picture

ornament   shelves *pl*   armchair   rug   cushion

Kitchens in the UK often have a table where you can eat.

VOCABULARY

to cook	to roast	to clean
to boil	to bake	

GENERAL

aluminium foil

apron

bin bag

clingfilm

kitchen roll

tea towel

to fry

to stir fry

to wash up

baking tray

cafetière

casserole dish

chopping board

colander

cooker

cooker hood

corkscrew

food processor

frying pan

garlic press

grater

hand mixer

kettle

kitchen knife

ladle

masher

measuring jug

mixing bowl

peeler

rolling pin

saucepan

sieve

spatula

teapot

tin opener

toaster

whisk

wok

wooden spoon

KITCHEN

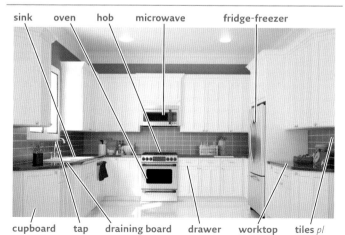

sink   oven   hob   microwave   fridge-freezer

cupboard   tap   draining board   drawer   worktop   tiles *pl*

It is good manners to wait until everyone has their food before you begin eating. It is also polite to wait for everyone to finish their meals before you leave the table.

GENERAL

coaster

dining table

napkin

pepper

place mat

salad bowl

salt

serving dish

vinegar

to clear the table

to eat

to set the table

TABLE SETTINGS

bowl

cup and saucer

cutlery

glass

knife and fork

plate

spoon

teaspoon

wine glass

VOCABULARY

master bedroom	en-suite bathroom	bedding
spare room	bed	to make the bed

GENERAL

alarm clock

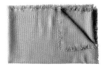

blanket

bunk beds *pl*

coat hanger

double bed

dressing table

hairdryer

laundry basket

nursery

quilt

sheets *pl*

single bed

to go to bed

to sleep

to wake up

BEDROOM

mirror   chest of drawers   wardrobe   duvet   curtains *pl*

drawer   bedside lamp   pillow   mattress   bedside table

THE BATHROOM

VOCABULARY

to have a shower   to go to the toilet

YOU SHOULD KNOW...

You cannot have electrical sockets in British bathrooms.

GENERAL

bath mat

face cloth

handwash

shower cap

shower curtain

soap

sponge

toilet brush

toilet roll

toothbrush

toothpaste

towel

to brush your teeth

to have a bath

to wash your hands

BATHROOM

mirror · sink · shower · toilet

tap · cabinet · bidet · bath

VOCABULARY

soil	plant	flower
grass	tree	to grow

GENERAL

allotment

compost

decking

gardener

garden fork

garden hose

gardening gloves *pl*

garden shed

greenhouse

hoe

lawnmower

plant pot

pruners *pl*

spade

Strimmer®

trowel

watering can

Wellington boots *pl*

wheelbarrow

window box

to mow the lawn

to plant

to water the plants

lawn shrub gate fence bird box

path flowers *pl* patio flowerpot

VOCABULARY

recycling bin	to do the laundry	to tidy up
to sweep the floor	to hoover	to clean

YOU SHOULD KNOW...

In the UK, different coloured bins are used for different types of waste.

bin

bleach

brush and dustpan

bucket

cloth

clothes horse

clothes pegs *pl*

dishwasher

dishwasher tablet

iron

ironing board

laundry detergent

mop

rubber gloves *pl*

scourer

tea towel

tumble drier

vacuum cleaner

washing line

washing machine

washing-up liquid

AT THE SHOPS

There are lots of places to shop in the UK. You can go shopping in local high streets where there are attractive small shops, buy fresh food at farmers' markets, and visit the many large shopping centres where you can find all the well-known shops.

basket

banana

bread

vegetable oil

Most shops in the UK are open seven days a week. Many have shorter hours at weekends, especially on Sundays. In big cities you can find 24-hour supermarkets.

YOU MIGHT SAY...

Where is the...?	Can I use contactless?
Where is the nearest...?	How much does this cost?
Where can I buy...?	How much is delivery?
What time do you open/close?	I need...
I'm just looking.	I would like...
Do you sell...?	I'd like to exchange this.
May I have...?	Can I get a refund?
Can I pay by cash/card?	That's all, thank you.

YOU MIGHT HEAR...

Are you being served?	Can you enter your PIN?
Can I help you?	Would you like a receipt?
Would you like anything else?	We don't offer refunds.
It costs...	Have you got a receipt?
I'm sorry, we don't have...	Have a good day!

YOU SHOULD KNOW...

Single-use plastic bags are available from most shops, but you have to pay for them. However, many people use their own bags or buy reusable bags.

shop	PIN	loyalty card
corner shop	exchange	to buy
customer	refund	to pay
cash	voucher	to order
change	gift voucher	

basket

card reader

counter

debit/credit card

market

paper bag

67

plastic bag

receipt

retail park

reusable shopping
bag

shop assistant

shopping centre

supermarket

till

trolley

to go shopping

to pay using
contactless

to shop online

Shopping online is very popular in the UK. Most supermarkets will deliver your shopping to your house.

YOU MIGHT SAY...	YOU MIGHT HEAR...
Where can I find...?	We have/don't have...
I'm looking for...	It's in aisle 1/2/3.
Do you have...?	You have to pay for plastic bags.
Can I have a plastic bag?	Do you have a loyalty card?

VOCABULARY

fresh   frozen   low-fat

GENERAL

aisle

bottle

box

carton

jar

tin

breakfast cereal

cooking sauce

couscous

flour

herbs *pl*

honey

icing sugar

instant coffee

jam

ketchup

marmalade

mayonnaise

mustard

noodles *pl*

olive oil

pasta

pepper

rice

salt

spices *pl*

sugar

teabags *pl*

vegetable oil

vinegar

SNACKS

biscuits *pl*

chocolate

crisps *pl*

nuts *pl*

popcorn

sweets *pl*

DRINKS

beer

fizzy drink

fruit juice

mineral water

spirits *pl*

wine

MARKET

You can find markets in towns and cities all across the UK. There are also farmers' markets in many villages, and car-boot sales at weekends.

YOU MIGHT SAY...

When is market day?

Do you have...?

What do I owe you?

YOU MIGHT HEAR...

The market is on a Tuesday.

What would you like?

Here's your change.

VOCABULARY

stall

produce

local

organic

seasonal

home-made

car-boot sale

farmer's market

flea market

indoor market

market

market trader

FRUIT AND VEGETABLES

VOCABULARY

juice	rotten	unripe
fresh	ripe	seedless

GENERAL

leaf

peel

pips *pl*

rind

skin

stone

FRUIT

apple

apricot

avocado

banana

blackberry

blackcurrant

blueberry

cherry

gooseberry

grape

grapefruit

kiwi fruit

lemon

lime

mango

melon

nectarine

orange

peach

pear

pineapple

plum

raspberry

redcurrant

rhubarb

strawberry

watermelon

asparagus

aubergine

broccoli

Brussels sprout

cabbage

carrot

cauliflower

celery

chilli

courgette

cucumber

garlic

green beans *pl*

leek

lettuce

mushroom

onion

peas *pl*

potato

red pepper

spinach

sweetcorn

tomato

turnip

FISHMONGER'S

VOCABULARY

fishmonger	scales *pl*	smoked
seafood	farmed	deboned
fillet	wild	

GENERAL

(fish)bone

shell

shellfish

FISH

anchovies *pl*

cod

haddock

79

herring

lemon sole

mackerel

monkfish

plaice

pollock

salmon

sardine

sea bass

trout

tuna

turbot

crab

crayfish

lobster

mussel

oyster

prawn

shrimp

scallop

squid

A kilo/slice of...

Can you slice this for me, please?

How much/many would you like?

I'd recommend...

VOCABULARY

meat	lamb	liver
fillet	chicken	cooked
beef	duck	raw
pork	turkey	free-range

GENERAL

butcher

red meat

white meat

TYPES OF MEAT

bacon

burger

chicken breast

chop

(cured) sausage

ham

joint

mince

pâté

sausages *pl*

ribs *pl*

steak

Many British bakeries sell sandwiches, as well as cakes, fresh bread, and rolls.

YOU MIGHT SAY...

Do you sell...?

Could I have...?

How much are...?

YOU MIGHT HEAR...

Who's next?

Would you like anything else?

It costs...

VOCABULARY

baker

white bread

brown bread

loaf

slice

pastry

gluten-free

to bake

SWEET

bun

cookie

cupcake

Danish pastry

doughnut

éclair

muffin

pancake

scone

baguette

(bread) rolls *pl*

croissant

crumpet

pasty

sandwich

sausage roll

savoury pie

sliced bread

FRESH AND DAIRY PRODUCTS

YOU SHOULD KNOW...

The colour on the top of a milk bottle shows you what type of milk is inside.

GENERAL

butter

cream

eggs *pl*

margarine

semi-skimmed milk

skimmed milk

soymilk

whole milk

yoghurt

86

brie

cheddar

cottage cheese

cream cheese

Edam

feta

goat's cheese

mozzarella

parmesan

Red Leicester

Stilton®

Wensleydale

PHARMACY

Pharmacies (sometimes called "chemist's") can also be found in some supermarkets in the UK.

YOU MIGHT SAY...

I need something for...

I'm allergic to...

I'm collecting a prescription.

What would you recommend?

Is this suitable for young children?

YOU MIGHT HEAR...

Do you have a prescription?

Do you pay for your prescription?

Do you have any allergies?

You should see a doctor.

I'd recommend...

YOU SHOULD KNOW...

You can only get antibiotics from a pharmacy with a prescription from a doctor. Prescriptions are free for everyone in Scotland, Wales, and Northern Ireland; in England you should check if you need to pay.

VOCABULARY

pharmacist	painkiller	hay fever
prescription	cold	stomach ache
antibiotics pl	the flu	headache
antihistamine	diarrhoea	sore throat
antiseptic	allergy	

bandage

condom

cough mixture

cream

drops *pl*

inhaler

insect repellent

medicine

plaster

suntan lotion

tablet/pill

tissues *pl*

antiperspirant

conditioner

handwash

mouthwash

razor

sanitary towel

shampoo

shaving foam

shower gel

tampon

toothbrush

toothpaste

blusher

comb

eyeshadow

foundation

hairbrush

hairspray

lip balm

lipstick

make-up

mascara

nail varnish

powder

VOCABULARY

disposable/reusable nappy	nappy rash	to be teething
	teething gel	to breast-feed
nappy sack		

CLOTHING

Babygro®/sleepsuit

bib

bootees *pl*

mittens *pl*

snowsuit

vest

HEALTH AND HYGIENE

baby food

baby lotion

baby's bottle

changing bag

cotton buds *pl*

cotton wool

formula milk

nappy

nappy cream

powder

rusk

wet wipes *pl*

ACCESSORIES

baby bath

baby seat

baby sling

baby walker

cot

dummy

highchair

mobile

Moses basket

potty

pram

pushchair

sterilizer

teething ring

travel cot

As well as newspapers and magazines, newsagents in the UK usually sell stationery, stamps, lottery tickets, and scratch cards.

VOCABULARY

book of stamps

to play the lottery

to smoke

GENERAL

cigar

cigarette

comic book

confectionery

e-cigarette

envelope

greetings card

kiosk

lottery ticket

magazine

map

newspaper

notebook

pen

pencil

postcard

puzzle book

scratch card

stamp

stationery

tobacco

DEPARTMENT STORE

There are lots of department stores in the UK. These sell all kinds of different products.

YOU MIGHT SAY...

Where is the ... department?

Which floor is this?

Can you gift-wrap this, please?

Are there any toilets in the store?

YOU MIGHT HEAR...

It is on the second floor.

This is the first floor.

Would you like this gift-wrapped?

The lift is over there.

VOCABULARY

counter

department

floor

sale

womenswear

menswear

sportswear

swimwear

YOU SHOULD KNOW...

In the UK, the ground floor is the same as the first floor in some other countries; the first floor is the same as the second floor, and so on.

GENERAL

escalator

lift

toilets *pl*

accessories *pl*

cosmetics *pl*

electrical goods *pl*

fashion

food and drink

footwear

furniture

kitchenware

lighting

lingerie

soft furnishings *pl*

toys *pl*

CLOTHING AND FOOTWEAR

In the UK, you can find all your favourite international fashion shops as well as some British ones you may not know. Many people now also buy their clothes online.

YOU MIGHT SAY...

I'm just looking, thank you.

I'd like to try this on, please.

Where are the fitting rooms?

I'm a size...

Have you got this in...?

This is too...

YOU MIGHT HEAR...

Can I help you?

Let me know if I can help.

What size are you?

I'm sorry, we don't have any.

I can get you another size.

YOU SHOULD KNOW...

Clothing and shoe sizes in the UK are different from those in other countries.

VOCABULARY

clothes *pl*	cotton	plus-size
shoes *pl*	leather	to try on
wool	petite	to fit

GENERAL

fitting room

sale

size

99

bikini

blouse

boxer shorts *pl*

bra

cardigan

coat

dress

dressing gown

jacket

jeans *pl*

jogging bottoms *pl*

jumper

knickers *pl*

leggings *pl*

pyjamas *pl*

shirt

shorts *pl*

skirt

socks *pl*

sweatshirt

swimsuit

(three-piece) suit

tie

tights *pl*

trousers *pl*

T-shirt

waterproof jacket

ACCESSORIES

baseball cap

belt

bracelet

earrings *pl*

fragrance

gloves *pl*

handbag

jewellery

necklace

purse

scarf

umbrella

wallet

watch

woolly hat

FOOTWEAR

boots *pl*

high heels *pl*

lace-up shoes *pl*

sandals *pl*

slippers *pl*

trainers *pl*

DIY STORE

DIY is popular in the UK; small shops or large stores will sell what you may need.

VOCABULARY

home improvements *pl*	tool	toolbox
hardware shop	power tool	to do DIY

SKILLS

painting and decorating

plumbing

woodwork

EQUIPMENT

chisel

electric drill

hammer

nails *pl*

nuts and bolts *pl*

paint

paintbrush

paint roller

pliers *pl*

saw

screwdriver

screws *pl*

spanner

spirit level

stepladder

tiles *pl*

wallpaper

wrench

GARDEN CENTRE

The local garden centre is often a nice place to visit at the weekend. People choose plants and look at garden furniture and equipment, and then many like to relax in the café with afternoon tea. Many garden centres also sell clothing and gifts.

GENERAL

afternoon tea

bedding plant

compost

garden centre

garden furniture

hanging basket

parasol

planter

seeds *pl*

antique shop

barber's

beauty salon

bookmaker's

bookshop

boutique

car showroom

charity shop

discount store

electrical retailer

estate agent's

florist's

furniture store

hairdresser's

health food shop

jeweller's

music shop

off-licence

optician's

pet shop

phone shop

shoe shop

toyshop

travel agent's

DAY-TO-DAY

Business meetings, meals with friends, or courses of study... whatever your schedule is while in the UK, you will want to talk about what you are doing from day to day.

tea (with milk)

cup

handle

saucer

YOU MIGHT SAY...

Where are you going?

What time do you finish?

What are you doing today?

Are you free on...?

Would you like to meet up?

When/Where do you want to meet?

YOU MIGHT HEAR...

I'm at work/uni.

I have a day off.

I'm going to...

I'll be back by...

I'll meet you at...

I can't meet up then, sorry

VOCABULARY

to arrive	to work	to go home

to get dressed	to go to bed	to leave

to meet friends	to study	to wake up

In the UK, breakfast is usually a small meal of cereal, toast, and tea or coffee. Some people like to have a cooked breakfast, often at the weekend. British people often drink their tea with cold milk, and sometimes a little sugar.

VOCABULARY

breakfast in bed	to have breakfast	to miss breakfast

DRINKS

coffee

hot chocolate

milk

orange juice

smoothie

tea (with milk)

FOOD

boiled egg

bread and butter

bread and jam

breakfast cereal

chocolate spread

continental breakfast

cooked breakfast

croissant

jam

marmalade

muesli

porridge

scrambled eggs *pl*

toast

yoghurt

The evening meal is the main meal of the day for most people in the UK. This meal can be called either dinner, tea, or supper, depending on where you live in the UK. Lunch is often quite small, for example, sandwiches, salad, or soup.

YOU MIGHT SAY...

What's for dinner?
May I have...?

YOU MIGHT HEAR...

Dinner's ready!
Would you like...?

VOCABULARY

to have lunch | to have dinner/tea/supper

YOU SHOULD KNOW...

Afternoon tea is usually made up of tea, sandwiches, and cakes.

GENERAL

afternoon tea

dinner

lunch

to drink

to eat

to have a snack

breaded camembert

garlic bread

olives *pl*

pakora

pâté

prawn cocktail

quiche

smoked salmon

soup

baked beans *pl*

cauliflower cheese

chips *pl*

coleslaw

cooked vegetables *pl*

green salad

mashed potato

onion rings *pl*

peas *pl*

potatoes *pl*

rice

Yorkshire puddings *pl*

chicken tikka masala

cottage pie

fish and chips

haggis

Irish stew

Lancashire hotpot

pea and ham soup

ploughman's lunch

roast dinner

sausage and mash

steak and kidney pie

Welsh rarebit

apple pie

Bakewell tart

cheesecake

chocolate cake

crumble

custard

ice cream

meringue

rice pudding

sticky toffee
pudding

trifle

Victoria sponge

EATING OUT

Restaurants in the UK offer many different foods from around the world, so it's usually easy to find something that you like to eat. It is best to book a table before you go out, especially if you are going to a restaurant.

YOU MIGHT SAY...

I'd like to reserve a table.

A table for four, please.

We're ready to order.

What would you recommend?

What are the specials today?

May I have ..., please?

Do you have vegetarian/vegan options?

I'm allergic to...

Excuse me, this is cold.

This is not what I ordered.

May we have the bill, please?

YOU MIGHT HEAR...

At what time?

For how many people?

Sorry, we're fully booked.

Would you like anything to drink?

Are you ready to order?

I would recommend...

The specials today are...

Enjoy your meal!

VOCABULARY

set menu	gluten-free	to order
vegetarian	dairy-free	to ask for the bill
vegan	to reserve a table	to leave a tip

YOU SHOULD KNOW...

Many people leave some money for the waiter or waitress. This is called a tip. In the UK a tip is usually about 10% of the bill.

café

pub

restaurant

GENERAL

bar

beer garden

bill

bread basket

chair

cheese knife

condiments *pl*

(daily) specials *pl*

fish knife

jug of water

menu

napkin

salt and pepper

steak knife

table

tablecloth

tip

toothpicks *pl*

vinegar and oil

waiter/waitress

wine glass

FAST FOOD

Most larger British towns and cities have lots of different fast-food and takeaway restaurants. Online food delivery services also make it easy to order meals to enjoy at home.

YOU MIGHT SAY...

I'd like to order, please.

Do you deliver?

I'm sitting in/taking away.

How long will it be?

That's everything, thanks.

YOU MIGHT HEAR...

Can I help you?

Sit-in or takeaway?

We deliver/don't deliver.

Would you like anything else?

Small, medium, or large?

VOCABULARY

street food	to sit in	to order (online)
drive-thru	to take away	to place an order
an order to go/ a takeaway	to deliver	to collect an order

PLACES TO EAT

burger/snack van

fast-food chain

fish and chip shop

burger

chips *pl*

filled baguette

fish and chips

hot dog

kebab

noodles *pl*

pizza

sandwich

sushi

toasted sandwich

wrap

COMMUNICATION AND IT

Technology is an important part of our everyday lives. It helps us to stay in touch with friends and family, know what's going on, and find the information we need.

YOU MIGHT SAY/HEAR...

I'll give you a call later.

I'll text/email you.

What's your number?

This is a bad line.

I don't have any signal/WiFi.

What's your email address?

The website address is...

What's the WiFi password?

It's all one word.

It's upper/lower case.

VOCABULARY

post	app	to make a phone call
social media	battery	to post (online)
email	cable	to download/upload
email address	data	to charge your phone
internet	mobile phone	
WiFi	landline	to switch on/off
website	text message	to click/double-click on
link	phone signal	
icon	voice mail	to crash

YOU SHOULD KNOW...

The QWERTY keyboard is used in the UK.

charger

mouse mat

SIM card

smartphone

tablet

wireless router

COMPUTER

screen

tower

button

keyboard

mouse

Children start school at age 4-5 and can leave at age 16. England, Scotland, Wales, and Northern Ireland all have different education systems.

YOU MIGHT SAY...	YOU MIGHT HEAR...
What are you studying?	**I'm studying...**
What year are you in?	**I'm in Year 6/my final year.**

VOCABULARY

nursery school	headteacher	homework
primary school	playground	exam
secondary school	interactive whiteboard	degree
university	timetable	student union
college	lesson	student card
pupil	lecture	to learn
teacher	tutorial	to revise

YOU SHOULD KNOW...

School is usually from 9 a.m. to 3 p.m. Most pupils must wear school uniform.

SCHOOL UNIFORM

blazer

school uniform

tie

canteen/cafeteria

classroom

playing field

to sit an exam

to study

to teach

SCHOOL

colouring pencils *pl*

eraser

exercise book

paper

pen

pencil

pencil case

ruler

schoolbag

sharpener

textbook

whiteboard

HIGHER EDUCATION

campus

halls of residence *pl*

lecture hall

lecturer

library

student

YOU MIGHT SAY/HEAR...

Can we have a meeting?	I have a meeting with...
May I speak to...?	I'll email the files to you.
Who's calling?	Mr/Ms ... is on the phone.
Can I call you back?	Here's my business card.

YOU SHOULD KNOW...

It's quite normal for workers in many British offices to eat at their desks or work through their lunch break.

VOCABULARY

manager	figures *pl*	file
staff *pl*	meeting	attachment
colleague	presentation	username
client	report	password
human resources/HR	conference call	to type
salary	video conference	to log on/off
accounts *pl*	inbox	

business card

calculator

desk

desk lamp

filing cabinet

folder

hole punch

ink cartridge

in/out tray

laptop

notepad

paper clip

photocopier

printer

ring binder

scanner

scissors *pl*

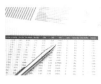

spreadsheet

stapler

sticky notes *pl*

sticky tape

swivel chair

telephone

USB stick

**to give a
presentation**

to have a meeting

to make a video call

THE BANK

Most banks are open during normal business hours from Monday to Friday, and some are also open on Saturday mornings.

YOU MIGHT SAY...

I'd like to...

... open an account.

... exchange some money.

Is there a fee for this service?

I need to cancel my debit/credit card.

YOU MIGHT HEAR...

May I see your ID, please?

How much would you like to withdraw/deposit?

Could you enter your PIN, please?

You must fill out a form.

You will have to make an appointment.

VOCABULARY

branch	account number	loan
PIN	sort code	mortgage
online banking	bank balance	interest
bank account	overdraft	to borrow
current account	bank transfer	to repay
savings account	currency	

ATM

banknotes *pl*

bank statement

bureau de change

cashier

chequebook

debit/credit card

exchange rate

safety deposit box

to change money

to make a deposit

to withdraw money

Post offices can sometimes be found inside other shops, for example, in newsagents.

YOU MIGHT SAY...

I'd like to send this first-class/ by airmail.

How long will delivery take?

I'd like a book of stamps, please.

YOU MIGHT HEAR...

Place it on the scales, please.

What are the contents?

What is the value of this parcel?

How many stamps do you need?

VOCABULARY

address	postwoman	airmail
postcode	courier	first-class
postman	mail	second-class

YOU SHOULD KNOW...

Postboxes in the UK are red, but you may see gold postboxes in some towns and cities – these celebrate gold medals won by local athletes at the 2012 London Olympic and Paralympic Games®.

GENERAL

box

delivery card

envelope

letter

package

padded envelope

parcel tape

postbox

postcard

postal worker

stamp

to post

to send by airmail

to sign for

IN TOWN

When you are in the UK, there are many places that you might need or want to visit. Some of the main ones are shown here.

YOU MIGHT SAY...

How do I get to...?

I need to go to...

I'd like to visit...

What are the opening hours?

YOU MIGHT HEAR...

It's open between ... and...

It's here on the map.

Ask at the tourist office.

It's closed on Sundays.

PLACES OF IMPORTANCE

café

cathedral

church

conference centre

courthouse

fire station

fountain

hospital

hotel

laundrette

library

mosque

office block

park

playground

police station

synagogue

town hall

LEISURE

A day trip, a weekend away, a night out, maybe even a night in – we all like to do different things in our free time. We also like to talk with friends and colleagues about our holidays and hobbies, or what we did at the weekend.

tent

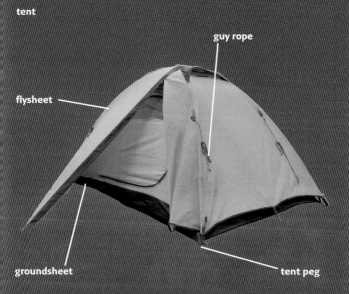

guy rope

flysheet

groundsheet

tent peg

British people like to do different things with their free time; favourite things to do include playing sport, going out, or having a quiet night in with a good book!

YOU MIGHT SAY...

What would you like to do?

What do you do in your spare time?

Have you got any hobbies?

Do you enjoy...?

Are you going on holiday this year?

YOU MIGHT HEAR...

My hobbies are...

I like...

I really enjoy it.

It's not for me.

I'm going to ... on holiday.

I don't have a lot of spare time.

VOCABULARY

spare time	holiday	exciting
activity	fun	relaxing
hobby	boring	interesting

GENERAL

to be bored

to enjoy

to relax

cooking

DIY

gaming

gardening

jogging

listening to music

reading

shopping

sport

travelling

walking

watching TV/films

SIGHTSEEING

Tourists from all over the world come to the UK every year. They visit the UK's exciting cities and beautiful countryside.

YOU MIGHT SAY...	YOU MIGHT HEAR...
How much is it to get in?	Entry costs...
Is there a discount for...?	There is/isn't a discount.
Where is the tourist office?	The tourist office is located...
Are there sightseeing tours?	You can book a guided tour.
Are there audio guides available?	Audio guides are/are not available.

VOCABULARY

tourist attraction	nature reserve	to visit
excursion	historic site	to see

YOU SHOULD KNOW...

Some cultural and historical sites, such as museums, art galleries, and stately homes, offer discounts for certain visitors.

art gallery

audio guide

camera

castle

cathedral

city map

gardens *pl*

guidebook

guided tour

monument

museum

sightseeing bus

tour guide

tourist

tourist office

EVENINGS OUT

There are lots of things to do in the evenings in most UK towns and cities. Ask what's on at the tourist office, or ask people who live there where they like to go.

YOU MIGHT SAY...

What is there to do at night?

What's on at the cinema/ theatre?

Where are the best bars/clubs?

Do you want to go for a drink?

Do you want to go and see a film/show?

Are there tickets for...?

Two seats in the stalls/balcony, please.

What time does it start?

YOU MIGHT HEAR...

There is/isn't a lot to do here.

My favourite bar/club is...

I'm going for a few drinks/to the theatre.

There's a film/show I'd like to see.

There are tickets/no tickets left.

It begins at 7 o'clock.

Please turn off your mobile phones.

VOCABULARY

a drink	to socialize	to watch a film
party	to enjoy yourself	to go dancing
film	to see a show	to order food/drinks

YOU SHOULD KNOW...

Restaurants in the UK do not usually stay open as late as they do in other parts of the world.

balcony

ballet

bar

box

box office

casino

cinema

comedy show

concert

festival

funfair

karaoke

musical

nightclub

opera

play

restaurant

stalls

theatre

HOTEL

There are plenty of places to stay in the UK. You can stay in a boutique hotel, a cosy bed and breakfast, or a cheap youth hostel.

Have you got any rooms available?

What time do I have to check out?

How much is it per night?

What time is breakfast served?

Is breakfast included?

I need fresh towels for my room.

I'd like to check in/out, please.

I'm in room number...

I have a reservation.

I've lost my key.

I'd like to book a single/double room, please.

I'd like to make a complaint.

YOU MIGHT HEAR...

We have some/don't have any rooms available.

May I have your room number, please?

Our rates are...

May I see your documents, please?

Breakfast is/is not included.

You may check in after...

Breakfast is served at...

You must check out before...

YOU SHOULD KNOW...

There are plans to introduce a tourist tax in some places across the UK.

VOCABULARY

bed and breakfast	wake-up call	to check out
full board	per person per night	to order room service
half board	to check in	

PLACES TO STAY

guesthouse

hotel

youth hostel

GENERAL

corridor

"do not disturb" sign

double room

en-suite bathroom

key card

minibar

porter

reception

receptionist

room number

room service

safe

single room

twin room

toiletries *pl*

CAMPING

There are many campsites all around the UK. You can also try "wild camping", where you don't camp in a campsite. However, if you are planning to do this, you should ask the person who owns the place you want to camp for permission where possible.

YOU MIGHT SAY...

Is it OK to camp here?

Have you got spaces available?

I'd like to book for ... nights.

How much is it per night?

Where is/are...?

Is the water drinkable?

YOU MIGHT HEAR...

You can/can't put your tent up here.

We have some/don't have any spaces available.

It costs ... per night.

The toilets/showers are...

The water is/is not drinkable.

VOCABULARY

pitch	to camp	to take down a tent
glamping	to pitch a tent	to go caravanning

GENERAL

air bed

camping stove

campsite

caravan

cool box

electricity hook-up

foot pump

matches *pl*

motorhome

picnic blanket

rucksack

sleeping bag

tent

toilet/shower block

torch

THE BEACH

The UK is an island, so it has many colourful seaside towns and beaches, as well as high cliffs you can walk along.

YOU MIGHT SAY...

Is there a good beach nearby?

Is swimming permitted?

Is the water cold?

Can we hire...?

Help! Lifeguard!

YOU MIGHT HEAR...

This is a public/private beach.

Swimming is allowed/not allowed.

Swimming is/is not supervised.

The water is warm/cold.

VOCABULARY

sea	Blue Flag beach	to sunbathe
beach	"No swimming"	to swim

YOU SHOULD KNOW...

Not all UK beaches have lifeguards. A red-and-yellow flag means that there is a lifeguard on the beach. A red flag means it is dangerous to swim, and a yellow flag means that you should be very careful in the water.

GENERAL

beach ball

beach flag

beach hut

beach towel

bikini

bucket and spade

flip-flops *pl*

ice-cream van

lifeguard

promenade

sand

sandcastle

seashells *pl*

seaweed

sunglasses *pl*

sunhat

suntan lotion

sun umbrella

swimming trunks *pl*

swimsuit

windbreak

pier

sea

beach

deckchair

The UK has many music festivals throughout the year, from large concerts like Glastonbury, to smaller classical music festivals such as The Proms in London.

YOU MIGHT SAY...

I enjoy listening to music.

I'm learning to play the...

What kind of music do you like?

YOU MIGHT HEAR...

I like/don't like...

My favourite band is...

VOCABULARY

song	rap	to play an instrument
album	classical	to sing
live music	folk	to listen to music
pop	electronic	to go to gigs
rock	jazz	to stream music
hip-hop	country	

GENERAL

band

choir

conductor

DJ

gig

musician

orchestra

sheet music

singer

MUSICAL INSTRUMENTS

accordion

acoustic guitar

bagpipes *pl*

bass guitar

cello

clarinet

double bass

drum

electric guitar

flute

harp

keyboard

mouth organ

piano

saxophone

tambourine

trombone

trumpet

tuba

violin

xylophone

Bluetooth® speaker

CD

earphones *pl*

headphones *pl*

microphone

soundbar

speakers *pl*

turntable

vinyl record

Photography is a popular hobby in the UK. There are a lot of things to photograph, from beautiful scenery to exciting city landscapes.

YOU MIGHT SAY...

Can I take photos here?

Where can I print my photos?

YOU MIGHT HEAR...

Photography isn't allowed.

Say cheese!

VOCABULARY

photographer	selfie stick	to upload a photo
photo	landscape	to take a photo/selfie
selfie	portrait	to zoom in

camera lens

compact camera

drone

DSLR camera

SD card

tripod

Many people play board games at home. People also play other games like darts and cards in pubs. Many pubs have quiz nights when teams try to answer questions and win prizes.

YOU MIGHT SAY...

What would you like to play?

What are the rules?

How do you play?

YOU MIGHT HEAR...

Let's play a game of...

It's your turn.

Time's up!

VOCABULARY

player	hand (in cards)	to win
team	to play	to lose

GAMING

game controller

games console

gaming

joystick

video game

virtual reality headset

board game

bowling

cards *pl*

chess

counters *pl*

crossword

darts

dice

dominoes

draughts

jigsaw puzzle

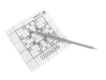

sudoku

VOCABULARY

knitting	dressmaker	to paint
sewing	artist	to sketch

GENERAL CRAFTS

embroidery

jewellery-making

model-making

papercrafts *pl*

pottery

woodwork

to crochet

to knit

to sew

canvas

easel

ink

oil paint

paintbrush

palette

paper

pastels *pl*

pen

pencil

sketchpad

watercolours *pl*

ball of wool

button

crochet hook

fabric

fabric scissors *pl*

knitting needles *pl*

needle and thread

pins *pl*

safety pin

sewing basket

sewing machine

tape measure

SPORT

People in the UK love watching and playing different sports, for example, football, rugby, tennis, and cricket. There are lots of sports and fitness clubs you can join, and many sporting events that you can watch. You may want to play a sport or go to the gym, or maybe just chat about your favourite team or sportsperson.

football pitch

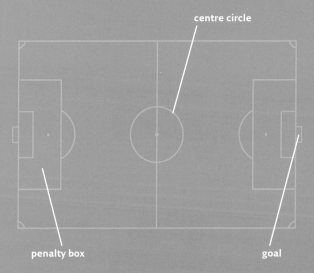

centre circle

penalty box

goal

YOU MIGHT SAY...

Where is the nearest...?

I play...

I'd like to book...

I support...

YOU MIGHT HEAR...

Do you do any sports?

What's your favourite team?

I'm a ... fan.

Who do you support?

VOCABULARY

player	points *pl*	to score
competition	score	to win
manager	to coach	to lose
match	to compete	to draw

coach

draw

leisure centre

medal

official

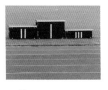

podium

referee

scoreboard

spectators *pl*

sportsperson

stadium

stands *pl*

team

teammate

trophy

AT THE GYM

YOU MIGHT SAY...

I'd like to join the gym.

I'd like to book a class.

What classes can you do here?

YOU MIGHT HEAR...

Are you a member here?

What time would you like to book for?

VOCABULARY

gym	personal trainer	to book
gym membership	exercise class	to go for a run
gym instructor	to exercise	to go to the gym

EXERCISES

Pilates

press-ups *pl*

running

sit-ups *pl*

spinning

yoga

changing room

cross trainer

dumbbell

exercise bike

gym ball

kettlebell

locker

rowing machine

showers *pl*

skipping rope

treadmill

weightlifting bench

FOOTBALL

Football is the most popular sport in the UK. There is no UK team; each country has its own national team. Many people support the team where they live, rather than one of the larger teams.

YOU MIGHT SAY...

Are you going to watch the match?

What's the score?

YOU MIGHT HEAR...

The score is...

Go on!

VOCABULARY

supporter	kick-off	offside
defender	half-time	foul
striker	full-time	to play football
substitute	free kick	to pass the ball

assistant referee

football

football boots *pl*

football match

football pitch

football player

goal

goalkeeper

goalkeeper's gloves *pl*

header

penalty kick

shin pads *pl*

tackle

whistle

yellow/red card

to kick the ball

to save

to score a goal

Rugby union and rugby league are both popular in the UK. The Six Nations tournament – with teams from England, Scotland, Ireland, Wales, France, and Italy – is in February and March every year.

VOCABULARY

forward	penalty kick	to play rugby
back	pass	to tackle
conversion	headguard	to score a try

mouthguard

rugby

rugby ball

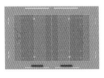

rugby field

rugby player

(rugby) posts *pl*

scrum

try

wheelchair rugby

CRICKET

Cricket is very popular in England. The most important competition is the Ashes tournament. It is played between the English and Australian national teams, and happens every two years.

VOCABULARY

batsman/batswoman	cricket pitch	run
bowler	innings	to play cricket
wicket-keeper	over	to score a run

cricket

cricket ball

cricket bat

cricket helmet

leg pads *pl*

wicket

to bat

to bowl

to field

People in the UK have played tennis since 1873, and today it is one of the most popular sports in the country.

VOCABULARY

ace	game, set and match	to play badminton/squash/tennis
fault	singles (match)	to hit
rally	doubles (match)	to serve
deuce		

YOU SHOULD KNOW...

Wimbledon started in 1877 and is the oldest tennis competition in the world.

GENERAL

backhand

forehand

serve

BADMINTON

badminton

badminton racket

shuttlecock

SQUASH

squash

squash ball

squash racket

TENNIS

ball boy/ball girl

line judge

net

tennis

tennis ball

tennis court

tennis player

tennis racket

umpire

VOCABULARY

swimming	to dive	to row
diving	to surf	to sail
to swim	to paddle	to fish

POOL

armbands *pl*

diver

diving board

flippers *pl*

goggles *pl*

lane

lifeguard

swimmer

swimming cap

swimming pool

swimming trunks *pl*

swimsuit

angler

bodyboarding

canoeing

fishing

fishing rod

jet ski®

kayaking

lifejacket

oars *pl*

paddle

paddleboarding

rowing

sailing

scuba diving

snorkelling

surfboard

surfer

surfing

waterskiing

wetsuit

windsurfing

There are a number of ski resorts in the Scottish Highlands, and excellent walking and climbing in areas such as the Peak District and Snowdonia.

YOU MIGHT SAY...

Can I hire some skis?

I'd like a skiing lesson, please.

What are the snow conditions like?

I've fallen.

YOU MIGHT HEAR...

You can hire skis here.

You can book a skiing lesson here.

The conditions are good/bad.

VOCABULARY

skier	ice rink	to go sledging
ski resort	mountain rescue service	to go ice skating
ski instructor		to go mountain climbing
snow	to ski	
ice	to snowboard	

GENERAL

avalanche

chair lift

curling

dry ski slope

ice skates *pl*

ice skating

salopettes *pl*

ski boots *pl*

ski gloves *pl*

ski goggles *pl*

ski helmet

ski jacket

ski lift

ski poles *pl*

skis *pl*

sledge

snowboard

snowboarding
boots *pl*

carabiner clip

compass

crampons *pl*

ice axe

map

rope

rucksack

walking boots *pl*

walking poles *pl*

VOCABULARY

martial arts *pl*	opponent	to punch
fight	to box	to kick
fighter	to wrestle	to knock out

GENERAL

belt

fencing sword

headguard

judo/karate suit

mouthguard

referee

BOXING

boxer

boxing gloves *pl*

boxing ring

boxing shoes *pl*

knockout

punchbag

OTHER COMBAT SPORTS

fencing

judo

karate

kickboxing

taekwondo

wrestling

VOCABULARY

runner	heat	to do athletics
race	final	to run
marathon	sprint	to race
start line	triple jump	to jump
finish line	indoor athletics	to throw

YOU SHOULD KNOW...

The modern Olympics® started in Athens in 1896, and the Paralympic movement started in England in 1948.

athlete

discus

high jump

hurdles

javelin

lane

long jump

pole vault

relay

running track

shot put

spikes *pl*

starter's gun

starting blocks *pl*

stopwatch

People say that the modern game of golf started in Scotland in the 15th century.

VOCABULARY

golfer	hole	over/under par
golf course	hole-in-one	to play golf
green	handicap	to tee off

bunker

caddie

clubhouse

golf bag

golf ball

golf buggy

golf club

putter

tee

American football

archery

baseball

basketball

BMX

bowls

climbing

gymnastics

hockey

horse racing

ice hockey

motorcycle racing

motor racing

netball

shooting

showjumping

skateboarding

snooker

table tennis

track cycling

triathlon

volleyball

water polo

weightlifting

HEALTH

It is best to be prepared for your visit to the UK. Make sure you have the correct healthcare cover, and if you are on holiday, you must have travel insurance.

first-aid kit

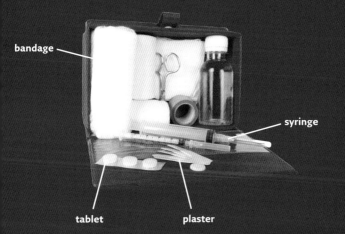

bandage

syringe

tablet

plaster

The National Health Service (NHS) provides free medical care for people who usually live in the UK. There are also many private hospitals and healthcare practices.

YOU MIGHT SAY...

I don't feel well.

I've hurt...

I need to see a doctor/go to hospital.

Can you call an ambulance?

YOU MIGHT HEAR...

What's wrong?

Where does it hurt?

What happened?

How long have you been feeling ill?

YOU SHOULD KNOW...

999 is the emergency number for the UK – use it to call the police, ambulance, or fire brigade. 111 is the number for non-emergency medical advice. You can ask for a translator when you call either number.

VOCABULARY

first aid	mental health	to hurt
illness	treatment	to recover
symptom	health insurance	to treat

EMERGENCY SERVICES

ambulance

fire brigade

police

doctor

first-aid kit

hospital

medicine

nurse

paramedic

patient

pharmacist

pharmacy

to be ill

to be in pain

to feel sick

VOCABULARY

tongue	breast	to touch
skin	height	to taste
(body) hair	weight	to stand
beard	to see	to walk
moustache	to smell	to move
genitals *pl*	to hear	

YOU SHOULD KNOW...

In English, the possessive adjective (for example, *my*, *his*, *their*) is generally used when talking about body parts. For instance, you say "We washed our hands" or "I've hurt my leg".

HEAD

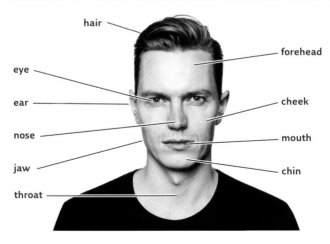

hair — forehead

eye

ear — cheek

nose — mouth

jaw — chin

throat

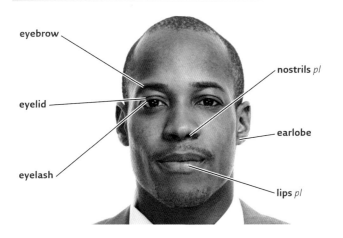

eyebrow

nostrils *pl*

eyelid

earlobe

eyelash

lips *pl*

HAND

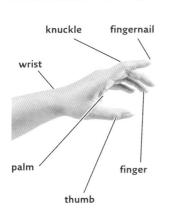

knuckle

fingernail

wrist

palm

finger

thumb

FOOT

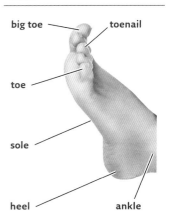

big toe

toenail

toe

sole

heel

ankle

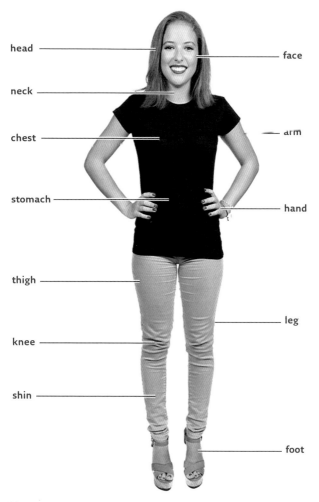

head

face

neck

arm

chest

stomach

hand

thigh

leg

knee

shin

foot

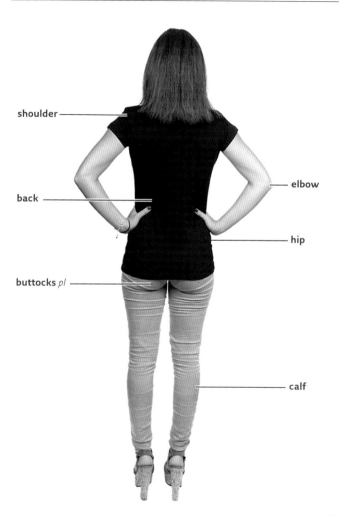

shoulder

elbow

back

hip

buttocks *pl*

calf

VOCABULARY

organ	muscle	cell
blood	nerve	artery
joint	tendon	vein
skeleton	tissue	oxygen
bone	ligament	

INTERNAL ORGANS

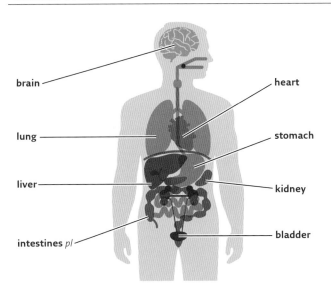

brain

heart

lung

stomach

liver

kidney

intestines *pl*

bladder

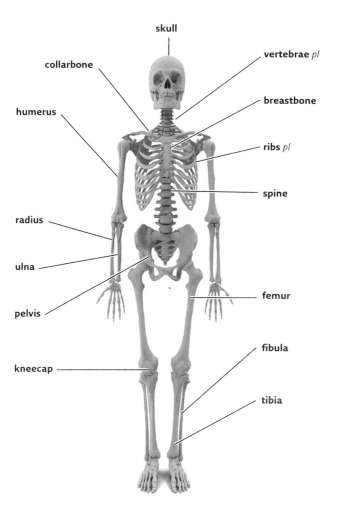

skull

collarbone

vertebrae *pl*

breastbone

humerus

ribs *pl*

spine

radius

ulna

pelvis

femur

kneecap

fibula

tibia

THE DOCTOR'S SURGERY

In the UK, you may wish to register with a local GP practice or a health centre. You will need to live near to the GP practice or health centre, and you must have proof of address and photo ID.

I'd like to register with the practice.

I'd like to make an appointment.

I have an appointment with Dr...

I'm allergic to...

I'm on medication for...

I've been feeling unwell.

The doctor will see you now.

What are your symptoms?

May I examine you?

Tell me if that hurts.

Do you have any allergies?

Do you take any medication?

Take two tablets twice a day.

VOCABULARY

health centre	test	sleeping pill
appointment	prescription	to make an appointment
clinic	antibiotics *pl*	
examination	insulin	to examine
		to be on medication

blood pressure monitor

examination room

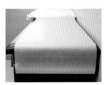

examination table

GP/doctor

medication

practice nurse

stethoscope

syringe

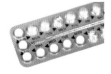

the pill

thermometer

vaccination

waiting room

THE DENTIST'S SURGERY

VOCABULARY

hygienist	filling	extraction
check-up	crown	toothache
wisdom teeth *pl*	root canal treatment	abscess

YOU SHOULD KNOW...

You usually have to pay for dental care in the UK.

GENERAL

braces *pl*

dental floss

dental nurse

dentist

dentist's chair

dentist's drill

dentures *pl*

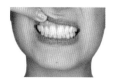
gums *pl*

mouthwash

teeth *pl*

toothbrush

toothpaste

to brush your teeth

to floss

to have toothache

THE OPTICIAN'S

VOCABULARY

reading glasses *pl*	cataracts *pl*	blind
lens	short-sighted	colour-blind
conjunctivitis	long-sighted	to wear glasses
blurred vision	visually impaired	to wear contacts

YOU SHOULD KNOW...

In most parts of the UK you have to pay for eye care, although it is free in Scotland.

GENERAL

contact lens case

contact lenses *pl*

eye chart

200

eye drops *pl*

eye test

frames *pl*

glasses *pl*

glasses case

guide dog

optician

ophthalmologist

stye

In the UK, hospitals see patients who are sent there by their GP, and help people in an emergency.

YOU MIGHT SAY...	YOU MIGHT HEAR...
Which ward is he/she in?	He/She is in ward...
When are visiting hours?	Visiting hours are from ... to...

VOCABULARY

patient	visiting hours *pl*	to have surgery
visitor	diagnosis	to be admitted/ discharged

YOU SHOULD KNOW ...

Treatment at a UK hospital is free at the moment of need. However, patients from other countries may need to pay for some hospital services.

A&E

crutches *pl*

defibrillator

drip

hospital bed

hospital trolley

intensive care

monitor

operating theatre

operation

oxygen mask

plaster cast

stitches *pl*

surgeon

ward

wheelchair

X-ray

Zimmer frame®

YOU MIGHT SAY...

I've had an accident.

I've hurt...

I've broken/sprained...

I've cut/burnt myself.

I've hit my head.

YOU MIGHT HEAR...

Do you feel faint?

Do you feel sick?

I'm calling an ambulance.

Where does it hurt?

Tell me what happened.

YOU SHOULD KNOW...

Ambulances in the UK are for serious accidents and emergencies only. If you hurt yourself, you should see a GP, or go to A&E at the nearest hospital.

VOCABULARY

accident	CPR	to injure yourself
concussion	recovery position	to fall
fall	pulse	to break your arm
whiplash	to be unconscious	to twist your ankle

GENERAL

to carry out CPR

to put someone into the recovery position

to take someone's pulse

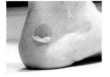

blister

bruise

burn

cut

dislocation

fracture

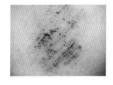

graze

scar

splinter

sting

sunburn

swelling

adhesive tape

antiseptic cream

bandage

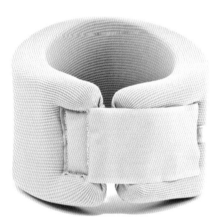

neck brace

dressing

ice pack

plaster

sling

tweezers *pl*

ILLNESS

YOU MIGHT SAY...

I have...

I'm going to be sick.

YOU MIGHT HEAR...

You should go to the doctor.

You need to rest.

VOCABULARY

heart attack	stomach bug	asthma
stroke	nausea	dizziness
infection	diarrhoea	to feel/be sick
the flu	constipation	to faint
migraine	diabetes	to have high/low blood pressure
virus	epilepsy	

chicken pox

fever

rash

to cough

to sneeze

to vomit

If you plan to have your baby in the UK, you will be able to see a midwife during your pregnancy.

YOU MIGHT SAY...

I'm/She's (six months) pregnant.

I'm/She's having contractions every ... minutes.

My/Her waters have broken.

YOU MIGHT HEAR...

How long is it between contractions?

May I examine you?

Push!

VOCABULARY

foetus	delivery	to be in labour
cervix	Caesarean section	to give birth
labour	miscarriage	to miscarry
gas and air	due date	to breast-feed
birth plan	to be pregnant	

YOU SHOULD KNOW...

A full-term pregnancy in the UK is 39 weeks and 6 days.

antenatal class

epidural

hospital tag

incubator

labour suite

midwife

morning sickness

newborn

pregnancy test

pregnant woman

sonographer

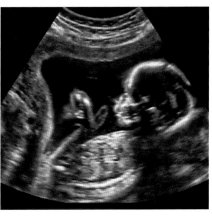

ultrasound

ALTERNATIVE THERAPIES

Alternative therapies are becoming popular in the UK, but you may have to pay for any treatments.

VOCABULARY

therapist	acupuncturist	reiki
masseur	reflexologist	to massage
masseuse	remedy	to meditate
chiropractor	supplements *pl*	

YOU SHOULD KNOW...

Going to a spa or health resort is popular with many British people who want to improve their health and wellbeing.

acupuncture

chiropractic

essential oil

herbal medicine

homeopathy

hypnotherapy

massage

meditation

osteopathy

sauna

reflexology

shiatsu massage

spa

steam room

traditional Chinese medicine

If you are going to travel to the UK with your pet, they must be microchipped, vaccinated against rabies, and have a pet passport. Dogs must get a tapeworm treatment from a vet 1–5 days before they enter the UK.

YOU MIGHT SAY...	YOU MIGHT HEAR...
My dog is hurt.	What is the problem?
My cat has been sick.	Is your pet microchipped?

VOCABULARY

pet passport	tapeworm treatment	to microchip
quarantine	tick	to spay/neuter
microchip	to worm	to put down

E-collar

flea

flea collar

pet carrier

vaccination

vet

PLANET EARTH

The UK has some beautiful places to visit. Choose from the mountains in Scotland and Wales, the coast of Northern Ireland, or the green hills of England. There are lots of walking routes so you can discover the country for yourself. Look out for the many nature reserves and national parks around the country too.

puffin

beak

wing

tail

claw

VOCABULARY

animal	species	to bark
bird	fur	to purr
fish	wool	to growl

beak

claw

feather

hoof

horns *pl*

mane

paw

tail

wing

DOMESTIC ANIMALS AND BIRDS

The UK is known for its love of animals. You can take your dog to many pubs and cafés. You should keep your dog on a lead on countryside walks, where there are sheep or cows.

YOU MIGHT SAY...

Do you have any pets?

Is it OK to bring my pet?

YOU MIGHT HEAR...

I'm allergic to pet hair.

Animals are not allowed.

VOCABULARY

farmer	barn	field
farm	hay	guide dog
owner	straw	

BABY ANIMALS AND BIRDS

calf

chick

foal

kitten

lamb

puppy

budgerigar

cat

dog

ferret

goldfish

guinea pig

hamster

parrot

pony

rabbit

rat

tropical fish

bull

chicken

cow

donkey

duck

goat

goose

horse

pig

sheep

sheepdog

turkey

aquarium

cage

catflap

collar

dog basket

hamster wheel

hutch

kennel

lead

litter tray

pet food

stable

alligator

chameleon

crocodile

frog

gecko

iguana

lizard

newt

snake

toad

tortoise

turtle

badger

bat

deer

fox

hare

hedgehog

mole

mouse

otter

squirrel

stag

weasel

OTHER COMMON MAMMALS

bear

camel

chimpanzee

elephant

giraffe

gorilla

hippopotamus

kangaroo

lion

monkey

rhinoceros

tiger

blackbird

crow

dove

eagle

falcon

finch

gannet

gull

hawk

heron

kingfisher

lark

ostrich

owl

peacock

pelican

penguin

pigeon

puffin

robin

sparrow

starling

swan

thrush

VOCABULARY

swarm	cobweb	to buzz
nest	insect bite	to sting

ant

bee

beetle

butterfly

caterpillar

cockroach

daddy longlegs

dragonfly

earthworm

earwig

fly

grasshopper

ladybird

midge

mosquito

moth

slug

snail

spider

wasp

woodlouse

crab

dolphin

eel

jellyfish

killer whale

lobster

octopus

seal

sea urchin

shark

starfish

whale

branch

bulb

leaf

petal

seeds *pl*

trunk

FLOWERS

bluebell

buttercup

carnation

daffodil

daisy

heather

hyacinth

iris

lily

orchid

pansy

poppy

rose

sunflower

tulip

PLANTS AND TREES

birch

cherry

clover

fir

fungus

ivy

maple

moss

nettle

oak

pine

poplar

sycamore

thistle

willow

VOCABULARY

landscape	water	rural
soil	air	urban

LAND

cave

desert

farmland

forest

glacier

hill

lake/loch

marsh

meadow

moorland

mountain

pond

river

rocks *pl*

stream

valley

volcano

waterfall

SEA

cliff

coast

island

peninsula

rock pool

sand dunes *pl*

SKY

aurora

clouds *pl*

comet

moon

rainbow

stars *pl*

sun

sunrise

sunset

SPECIAL DAYS

Everyone loves being with friends and family on special days. In the UK, this usually means eating good food and maybe having a glass of champagne. Look out for all the local parties and activities you can take part in on the various holidays in the UK.

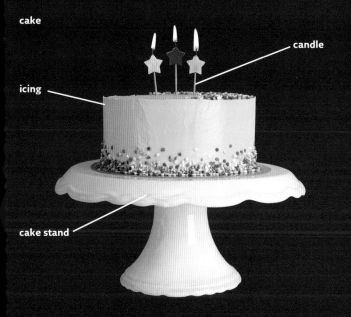

cake

candle

icing

cake stand

YOU MIGHT SAY/HEAR...

Congratulations!	Best wishes.
Well done!	Thank you.
Cheers!	You're very kind.
Happy birthday!	Cheers to you, too!
Happy anniversary!	

VOCABULARY

occasion	surprise party	good/bad news
celebration	wedding anniversary	to celebrate
birthday	bank/public holiday	to throw a party
birthday party	religious holiday	to make a toast

YOU SHOULD KNOW...

People in the UK love to buy greetings cards to give other people on a special day. In fact, they buy more greetings cards per year than anyone else in the world.

balloons *pl*

bouquet

box of chocolates

bunting

cake

champagne

confetti

decorations *pl*

fireworks *pl*

gift

gift bag

greetings card

party

streamers *pl*

toast

PUBLIC HOLIDAYS

There are between 8 and 10 official public holidays (also known as bank holidays) each year in the UK.

VOCABULARY

Mother's Day | Father's Day | May Day

YOU SHOULD KNOW...

On April Fool's Day (1st April), many people play tricks on each other and say 'April Fool!'

BRITISH CELEBRATIONS

Burns Night

ceilidh

Eisteddfod

Guy Fawkes Night

Irish dancing

Morris dancing

April Fool's Day

Chinese New Year

Diwali

Easter

Eid al-Fitr

Halloween

Hanukkah

Holi

Passover

Ramadan

Shrove Tuesday

Valentine's Day

Christmas is celebrated on December 25th in the UK with gifts and a special Christmas dinner. This is often roast turkey, with Christmas pudding for dessert. Boxing Day (December 26th) is also a public holiday.

YOU MIGHT SAY/HEAR...

Merry Christmas!

Happy New Year!

VOCABULARY

Advent	**Christmas Day**	**Christmas carol**
Christmas Eve	**Boxing Day**	**New Year's Day**

YOU SHOULD KNOW...

Many British people go to a pantomime around Christmas. Pantomimes are plays based on fairy tales, and include singing, dancing, and comedy. They are fun for all the family.

Advent calendar

bauble

carol singing

Christmas card

Christmas cracker

Christmas dinner

Christmas lights *pl*

Christmas pudding

Christmas tree

Father Christmas/ Santa Claus

mince pie

Nativity play

New Year's Eve/ Hogmanay

pantomime

present

tinsel

wrapping paper

wreath

People often give greetings cards on birthdays and other life events, happy or sad, in the UK. It is usual to celebrate someone's 18th and 21st birthdays.

VOCABULARY

first day of school	new job	moving house

baby shower

baptism/christening

bar/bat mitzvah

birth

engagement

funeral

graduation

retirement

wedding

VERBS

PHOTO CREDITS